★

A Day in the Life of a Midshipman

A Naval Institute Book for Young Readers

★

A Day in the Life
of a
Midshipman

Sandra Travis-Bildahl

With a Foreword by
Adm. William J. Crowe, Jr., USN (Ret.)

NAVAL INSTITUTE PRESS　　*Annapolis, Maryland*

Library of Congress Cataloging-in-Publication Data
Travis-Bildahl, Sandra, 1953–
    A day in the life of a midshipman / Sandra Travis-Bildahl; with a foreword
by William J. Crowe, Jr.
        p.   cm. — (A Naval Institute book for young readers)
    Summary: A midshipman's account of a typical day at the United States
Naval Academy portraying the dreams, aspirations, and hard work that
make up the four years spent there.
    ISBN 1-55750-823-2 (alk. paper)
    1. United States Naval Academy—Juvenile literature. [1. United States Naval
Academy. 2. Midshipmen.]   I. Title. II. Series.
V415.P1T73   1996
359'.0071'173—dc20   95-50504

Printed in the United States of America on acid-free paper ∞

03 02 01 00 99 98 97 96   9 8 7 6 5 4 3 2

First printing

Unless indicated otherwise, all photographs were taken by John Bildahl
and are used with his permission.

For Katy and Travis

★

And to all the midshipmen, Naval Academy personnel,
friends, and family who helped bring this book to life . . .
a special thank you.

★ ★ ★

Foreword

By the time I was nine years old, I had long been dreaming of becoming a naval officer. One of my earliest memories is of a picture of the USS *Pennsylvania* that hung over my bed. My father had been a radioman on the *Pennsylvania* when she escorted Woodrow Wilson to France in 1918, and our house was filled with memorabilia from that voyage. I pondered over all these mementos and read everything I could get my hands on about the Navy—history, biographies, adventure. One of the books I read, *Annapolis Today,* made one thing clear: I wanted to go to the Naval Academy in Annapolis. For a boy from Oklahoma City who'd never seen the ocean, the sea had somehow cast a spell over me—despite my landlocked existence.

A few years, and some sweat and tears later, I found myself headed for Annapolis to join the United States Naval Academy's Class of '47. The previous year at the University of Oklahoma had prepared me academically for the academy, but nothing prepared me for the atmosphere outside the classroom. As a midshipman, I had to get used to long hours standing watch, tough inspections, and—most of all—following orders, which wasn't my strong suit! However, I received an exceptional education, and despite some trials, my determination never wavered.

Probably the most important thing I took away from the academy was a strong set of lifelong friends. The camaraderie and good times we shared (sometimes in the most difficult of situations) made me grow up quickly and prepared me for a future in the Navy. I couldn't have asked for more from the "country club" on the Severn.

I hope this book will give you a good sense of the life of a midshipman and perhaps lead some of you to choose the Navy as a career. I would repeat my forty-seven years of service in a heartbeat if I had the chance.

ADM. WILLIAM J. CROWE, JR.
U.S. Ambassador to the United Kingdom
of Great Britain and Northern Ireland

The Naval Academy is a historic landmark located on 338 acres in Annapolis, Maryland. U.S. NAVAL ACADEMY

★ ★ ★

Behind the walls of the U.S. Naval Academy in Annapolis, Maryland, is a special world where everything has a purpose. It's a school where work is endless, the routine is tough, and the friendships last a lifetime.

The Naval Academy is a place where, among other things, you learn how to sail, navigate submarines, fly helicopters, even jump out of planes. And when it's all done, you're a leader and an officer in the U.S. Navy or Marine Corps.

I'm here to take you on a tour behind those walls. What you are about to read is a description of an average day in the life of a midshipman, like me. It's an inside look at a world you don't ordinarily get to see unless you live it.

Until now.

0630 Wake-Up

I grip the controls of my F-14A Tomcat fighter plane. Off my wing, I notice a fellow pilot, and nod. Just then the glare of the sun makes me close my eyes. And then it happens. My eyes won't open. I hear a loud ringing sound. I struggle. I'm about to crash . . .

Suddenly I wake up from my dream and remember, I'm Jonathan Wright, a second-class midshipman in my third year at the U.S. Naval Academy, and I've got one minute to get out of bed—or else.

An F-14 Tomcat soars across the sky. U.S. NAVAL INSTITUTE COLLECTION

Waking up isn't easy, but keeping your bed neat can be if you don't break (turn down) the sheets. Some midshipmen sleep on top of a perfectly made bed and use their own blanket to keep warm.

*"Mother B" is every midshipman's home at the Naval Academy.
Midshipmen can't go through the main doors (center)
until after they are commissioned.*

The reveille (wake up) bell rings. Together with more than four thousand midshipmen, I jump out of bed and turn on the bedroom lights. Everyone does the same thing, because if you don't, you might get fried (which means you're in trouble).

So begins the typical day for every midshipman at the Naval Academy. We all live together in Bancroft Hall, the largest dormitory in the United States to be built under one roof. It's named after George Bancroft, who founded the academy in 1845, but we've given it our own nickname. We call it "Mother B."

Inside, there are eight wings. That's a total of almost *five* miles of hallway and *thirty-three acres* of floor space! It's the kind of place where you can get lost. I remember when I first got here; I couldn't find my room. Racing down a hallway I ran into an upperclassman who demanded, "Where's your brace?" I couldn't imagine what a

About four thousand midshipmen attend the Naval Academy each year.
U.S. NAVAL ACADEMY

Life isn't easy for plebes; that's why they sometimes look nervous—or scared. U.S. NAVAL ACADEMY

brace was. I knew he didn't mean braces on my teeth or a knee brace for a leg injury. I was quickly shown that a brace is a way to hold your chin in tight against your neck. It's like trying to hold a pencil between your chest and your chin, but it's not easy for everyone. Some plebes have to try it over and over again.

At that moment I realized that finding my way around Bancroft Hall wasn't going to be as big a deal as finding my way around my new world, which even included a new language. That's because at the academy we use the Navy's words for things. For instance, beds are racks, floors are decks, bulkheads are walls, a scuttlebutt is a water fountain, the bathroom is a head, and chow is mealtime—one of our favorite words.

Anyway, I soon found my room among the 1,873 bedrooms (none of which is air-conditioned). Each of us shares a room with up to five other midshipmen. The rooms that hold four or more midshipmen are called barns.

When I first got here I was surprised at how small our rooms are. It's not always easy living in small quarters with a lot of people, but

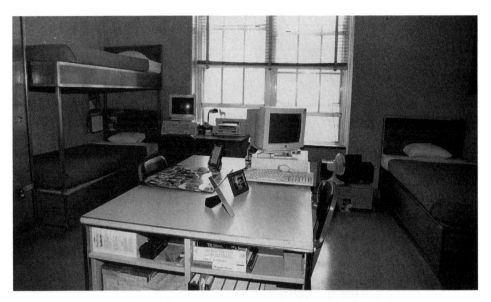

*Neatness counts when you're sharing a room with
two or more other midshipmen.*

we learn to work with each other. If our rooms get too noisy, we can go to the library to study.

(By the way, did you know Mother B has a secret room many midshipmen don't even know about? It's hidden behind a mirror that goes from the ground floor all the way to the roof.)

In Bancroft Hall we live in company areas. The entire brigade, all midshipmen, is divided into companies, each made up of about 120 young men and women. There are usually about thirty people from each class, or grade, in a company. Your company is like your team. We live together, drill together, compete together, and eat together. Being part of a company gives you a feeling for what your future life in the Navy and Marine Corps will be like. In those services you have to be good at working together in small groups.

Every company area in Bancroft Hall is kept shipshape. When we leave our rooms, window blinds must be at half-mast (halfway up, and open), and nothing can be adrift. In my closet the clothes are arranged with great care. My uniforms hang from left to right, black to white. My shoes are on a rack with the dark pairs on top

A midshipman tapes off his dark-colored uniform so no lint shows.

and the light ones on the bottom. No civvies (civilian clothes) are allowed in your closet until your last two years here.

I know where to find things fast. I learned how to do that plebe year (first year) when we had uniform races. The order was given, "You have two minutes to change from whiteworks (our white uniform) to winter working blues." From what I hear, changing into uniforms quickly is something that happens a lot in the military. I'm sure the day will come when I'll be in a deep sleep in my ship's bunk and be awakened with the command, "Up on the bridge now!" I won't have much time to get ready then.

What you wear has to look its best too. That's why I tape off my blue uniform. You take a big roll of tape, wrap it around your hand, and wipe off your dark clothes. The sticky part lifts off all the lint.

And now I'm ready for my day to begin.

0630 to 0700 Come-Arounds

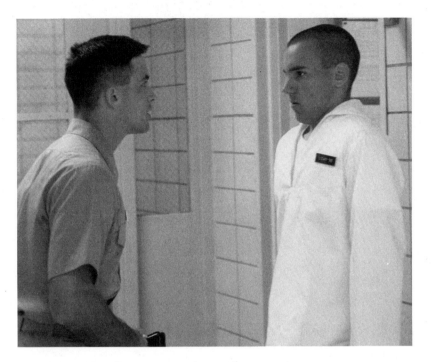

Come-arounds can be very *tense.*
U.S. NAVAL ACADEMY

It's time for come-arounds. That means a plebe will report to me, stand against the wall at attention, and answer my questions about military information. Every week we discuss a different topic, like Marine Corps and Navy history or strategy or naval etiquette.

For instance, if it's Marine Corps week, I might ask, "Name the crew on the M1-A1 Abrams tank." The answer? "Four crew members, sir. A tank commander, a gunner, a loader, and a driver." Or, I might ask, "When you're outside, what do you do when you hear colors (time for flag raising)?" The plebe should answer: "When the warning sounds for colors, you stop and come to attention. When the music for colors plays, you salute. When the last note sounds, you drop your salute. When you hear carry-on (go back to what you were doing) music, you can go on your way."

When midshipmen stand watch, they stay in position in hallways and enforce rules, answer phones in Mother B's main office, or raise the flag.

A trickier question might be, "What are the weapons forward to aft (front to back) on an *Oliver Hazard Perry*-class frigate?" Answer: "A Mk 13 missile launcher, six Mk 32 torpedo tubes, a Mk 76 75-millimeter gun, and a 20-millimeter CIWS (close-in weapons system)."

"What is the hull number of the ship?"

"FFG 7, sir."

Teaching each other like this is one of the special ways we learn at the academy. As they often say here, to be a leader you have to follow first.

Plebes can be rated (questioned) for up to half an hour. They stand at attention, their "eyes in the boat" (focused straight ahead).

That's why you take a lot of orders your first year, as a plebe. Second-year students, called third class or youngsters, train the plebes by quizzing them and making sure they're ready for the demands of the upper classes.

Third-year students (that's me), called second class, are responsible for overall plebe training. We're the ones who come down hard if plebes don't do things right.

Last-year students, called first class or firsties, make sure everything runs smoothly. They actually direct the brigade.

Being in charge can be tough. It's not easy to say to a friend: "You have to stand watch at the academy during Christmas vacation. That's an order!" (Standing watch can mean everything from raising the flag to answering phones in Bancroft Hall.)

Often I think about how these things prepare us for the future. I'm sure that if I'm out at sea some day on a dangerous mission, I'll appreciate what I learned here. I imagine it might be like this . . .

We're all focused on the jets arriving on the USS Enterprise, *our 1,123-foot, 90,000-ton nuclear aircraft carrier. It's high gear around here. If someone gives an order, I obey. Fast. There's no second-guessing in a situation like this. In minutes, a jet will land in an area the size of two football fields. On deck are four cables. The pilot must "catch" one of them to land the plane safely. If the jet crashes, the platform I'm standing on will collapse and I'll fall into a net that will take me under the deck. There I'll be safe from fire.*

Others wouldn't be so lucky. I feel my palms sweat, my breathing quicken, and my confidence soar. We've all been trained to be the best. In seconds, the jet lands. I relax. But just for a second. Here comes another one. And another . . .

Looking ahead is exciting. I can't wait until I graduate.

Precision landing really counts as this F-14 Tomcat returns to the aircraft carrier USS Independence. U.S. NAVAL INSTITUTE COLLECTION

0650 Chow Calls

Chow calls are made ten minutes and five minutes before formation.

From my room, I hear chow calls. That's when plebes stand in the halls of Mother B and yell out information like how much time we have before morning formation (when we all line up). They begin by calling out (*very* loudly), "Sir, you now have ten minutes until morning quarters formation . . ." Plebes also call out the location of formation, the uniform we will wear, the menu for the upcoming meal, and the names of the command duty officer and the officer of the watch for the day. Chow calls end with, "Sir, you now

*An upperclassman flames (puts pressures) on a plebe
while she does a chow call.*

have ten minutes, sir!" (Plebes also give a five-minute chow-call warning.)

Sometimes a mid (that's short for midshipman) from an upper class will flame (put pressure) on the plebes while they do chow calls. I can remember someone standing over me yelling, "Peanut butter, peanut butter, peanut butter." It can really throw you off when this happens, but that's the idea behind doing it.

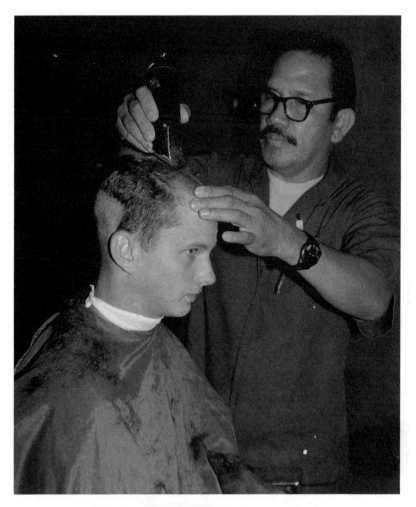

This is one way plebes get a new look.

Why? Because in the Navy, you need to know how to memorize and spit back facts under pressure, how to talk in a commanding voice and have a commanding presence no matter what's going on. Of course, chow calls are useful to us midshipmen because the plebes are passing on information we will need to know during the day.

The facts in chow calls are just a part of what we call daily rates, and plebes have to learn them by heart every day. They have to know things like how many days until Thanksgiving and Christmas,

Plebe summer begins with I-Day, when the plebes are inducted (opposite).
This day includes getting shots (above) *and haircuts, getting weighed and
measured, and signing up for a new life!* U.S. NAVAL ACADEMY

the names and times of all important events going on at the academy, as well as one sports-page and two front-page stories from the
newspaper. Except during meals and study hours, upperclass midshipmen can ask plebes their rates at any time.

No question about it, being a plebe is H-A-R-D.

When I first got here I was scared to death. I remember the first
day, after my parents left. I actually cried. And I wasn't the only
one. (One word about crying. DON'T! If you cry, the upperclass
mids won't let you forget it!)

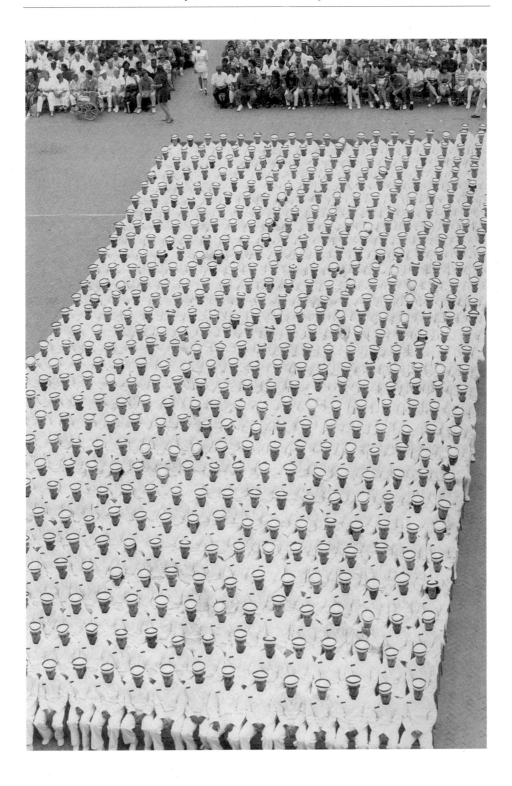

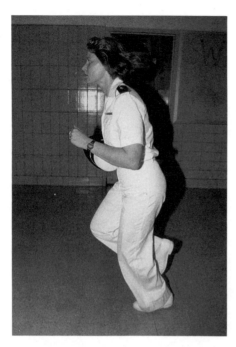

All plebes must chop (do double time) in Bancroft Hall.

All plebes must also square corners.

After this plebe squares this corner, he'll sound off,
yelling a phrase like "Go Navy, sir."

Plebes have to follow the most rules of all the midshipmen. For example, in Bancroft Hall plebes chop at all times, which is like running at attention. They square all corners (make a sharp turn), always run in the middle of the hallways, and go downstairs next to the bulkheads. There are certain ladders (stairways) they can't use. When plebes square corners, they sound off (shout), "Go Navy, sir," or "Beat Army, sir."

Plebes can't own a stereo, a Walkman, or a radio. They have to wear uniforms at the academy and in town at all times. They can't make friends with upperclass midshipmen. They can watch TV only certain hours at Dahlgren Hall. They aren't allowed to talk to classmates in the halls or stairways of Bancroft Hall, except under certain circumstances. They can never sit in the yard (campus). Plebes have to go to bed at certain hours, and the times they can leave the academy are very limited. Sounds like fun? It's not.

It's easy to see why one of my favorite memories is how plebe year ended. The tradition began in the early 1900s. It happens every year in May at the Herndon monument, which is greased with two hundred pounds of lard (fat) for the event. A dixie cup (the hat plebes wear during their first summer training) sits on top. The goal? To get that hat and replace it with the midshipman's cover (hat). It was just like this . . .

My legs shake as a fellow plebe climbs on my shoulders. I feel the pressure as someone else climbs on his shoulders. A pyramid of men and women, we sway in the wind. We fall. This isn't easy, and it hurts. Everyone's yelling. We've been trying to climb this twenty-one-foot obelisk for two hours. We're sweating and exhausted.

And then, we do it! One hat comes off and the other goes on. Everyone cheers.

I head back to Mother B with a group of my friends and we do everything we couldn't do as plebes. We touch the walls. We walk down the sides of the halls and we don't square corners. Wow! I'm not a plebe anymore. Nothing has ever felt better.

Herndon kicks off the big last week of the year, which ends with graduation. That's when the first-class graduates all throw their

The fastest Herndon climb was in 1969. It took only one minute and thirty seconds. In 1993 it took one hour, thirty-eight minutes, and twenty seconds. Midshipmen are getting slower: in 1995 it took four hours, five minutes, and seventeen seconds. U.S. NAVAL ACADEMY

Replacing the dixie cup (the plebes' summer cap). According to tradition, the midshipman who switches the hats will become the first member of the class to become an admiral. U.S. NAVAL ACADEMY

Commissioning day. For many midshipmen, their last day is their best day.
U.S. NAVAL ACADEMY

hats in the air. Midshipmen have been doing that since 1912. And the moment those hats go up, many of us put on our new shoulder boards to show that we've moved up a class. (Plebes are especially eager to move up.)

The stripes on your shoulder boards (or sleeves) show your rank. Every class has a rank represented by a certain number or placement of stripes. To find out what year a midshipman is in, you just have to look at the uniform.

So what's the purpose of ranks? It's an efficient way to communicate with four thousand people, and it's our way of knowing who's in charge. It's our chain of command. Around here, there's always someone higher in rank than you are making sure that whatever you're doing, you're doing it right!

After graduation, some say they'll never come back here because it's like a jail. Some say it's a great school to be *from,* but a terrible school to be *at.* Personally, I like it here (most of the time).

Another tradition around here is formation. If I don't hurry, I'll miss it.

0700 Formation

"Attention," calls a midshipman. The entire brigade is lined up in formation. A muster (roll call) is taken. Announcements are made.

As we stand together, I think about how we are all so different, but we all have something big in common. We're not just college students, we're midshipmen on active duty in the Navy. We're part of the military from the minute we take our oath of office when we're plebes. That means we promise to be loyal to our country and defend it if necessary. Each one of us will also serve in the military for six years after we graduate.

Marching in formation. U.S. NAVAL ACADEMY

The entire Brigade of Midshipmen is made up of two regiments, six battalions, and thirty-six companies. There are three platoons per company and three squads per platoon.

The service assignment process ends as midshipmen finalize their career choices. THE *LUCKY BAG*

We find out what we will do for those six years after going through something called service assignment. I'll start to go through the process next year, my last year.

It works like this. First you go through physicals. Navy medical personnel test and measure every part of your body: from the shoulder to the elbow, from the hip to the knee, from the knee to the heel, from the heel to the toe. They test your vision, your depth perception, your hearing, your teeth—everything! Then they tell you what you qualify for. For example, if you want to be a pilot, you've got to fit in a cockpit, be able to reach all the instruments, and have very good vision. I had a friend who wanted to be a pilot, but she was NPQ'D (not physically qualified). Luckily, she was qualified to be an NFO (naval flight officer), the person who sits behind or next to the pilot.

Once we know our options, we're interviewed by officers. At that time we express interest in the fields we want, but that still doesn't mean our wishes will come true. The big decision finally comes on a special service assignment day. We've worked and worked for this moment. We each get a number that puts us in a certain place in our class. That number is based on grades, athletic performance, behavior, and even how well we clean our rooms. Then we wait with our company until our number is called over the loudspeaker. For instance, we might hear "Zero to ninety-nine, line up"; we might also hear whispering like, "Pilot is taken."

That's why a lot of mids are incredibly tense during this process. Some of the hottest billets like pilot and Navy SEAL go fast. And if you don't get what you want, it means you worked four long years for a dream that isn't going to come true the way you hoped it would. Some midshipmen get pretty upset.

Of course, midshipmen can serve in lots of places. There are minesweepers and guided missile cruisers, helicopters and super-sonic jets on aircraft carriers, nuclear-powered attack and ballistic missile submarines. Or we can join the infantry and aviation units in the Marine Corps. And that's just a small sample of all the things we can do.

I think about where I might want to be in a few years. I try to imagine being on a submarine. I picture it like this . . .

> *As our nuclear-powered submarine dives down into the dark cold sea, I hear, "Lieutenant Wright, what's our position?" I chart our movements carefully. Navigation is crucial; our position is secret. Everyone is counting on me.*
>
> *We'll be under the ocean for over a month. I'm sure glad we have an ice cream machine on board.*

My daydreaming ends. My stomach growls. "Fall out," is called. It's time for breakfast.

Speaking of time, we tell time around here like they do in the military. We don't use A.M. and P.M. to describe morning and night. We just start at the beginning—0000 (midnight)—and go until 2359 (one minute before midnight).

The attack submarine USS Alexandria. U.S. NAVY

0715 Morning Meal

King Hall—the midshipmen mess—has more than 55,000 square feet of space. It's huge! U.S. NAVAL ACADEMY

Meals are served in King Hall to all four thousand of us in just five minutes! The cooks and bakers and galley (kitchen) staff are very efficient. They can cook three thousand hamburgers or a ton of shrimp an hour. They can roast 320 turkeys and heat 750 gallons of soup at once. On an average day, midshipmen drink more than 1,000 gallons of milk and eat 2 tons of potatoes, 1,200 loaves of bread, 720 pies, and 10,000 donuts!

Today we have the usual—coffee, hot chocolate, cold cereals, oatmeal, apple and orange juice—plus one of our favorites, the

This machine slices hundreds of loaves of bread.
That's why getting ready for a meal takes hours and hours.

MFSD (Midshipman Food Service Department) Waffle Kit. It's waffles topped with vanilla ice cream and strawberry syrup.

At meals we relax, but we also like to discuss military or political issues. For instance, I might ask: "How would you deploy (set up) a carrier battle group? Where would you put your ships? Submarines? Would you put your carriers in the center and your frigates in a circle around them for protection?" There are many interesting solutions.

We also watch our manners while we eat. We sit with napkins in our laps and always say please and thank you. We know that if someone asks for salt, you also pass the pepper.

Being polite is important here. Back at home people notice my manners. I remember what happened last spring break . . .

The galley—kitchen—staff can serve up four thousand hamburgers in just five minutes.

"Would you like some mashed potatoes?" asked my mom.

"Yes, ma'am," I answered. My sister rolled her eyes; my best friend from high school could hardly keep from laughing.

"What's so funny?" I asked.

"You," said my friend.

Before I could figure out what he meant, my Uncle Jack jumped in with a question. "Would you like to visit us tomorrow?"

"Yes, sir," I responded. Everyone laughed then, including me. I finally understood what was so funny. It was me.

"What's so funny?" someone asks. I realize I was a million miles away. Everyone's looking at me, including a polite plebe who is asking permission to leave the table. "Sir, excuse me, sir." I nod agreement as I finish my waffle. Then I excuse myself and head back to my room to hang out for a few minutes.

I don't get too many chances to relax here. This school is a real pressure cooker. If you add up everything you have to do, every day, it's like putting a ten-pound load in a two-pound bag. Everyone wants a piece of your time. The best way to cope is time management, but sometimes you just can't fit everything in. I admit I've become pretty efficient. I really see the changes in me when I go home on leave (vacation). It's hard to sit still; I feel like I've always got to accomplish something.

Going home also magnifies my feelings of separation from the world outside. Back home I think my friends have changed, but it's really me. In some ways it's a relief to get back to Annapolis. No one else understands what we go through here.

Which reminds me of something. Classes! My few minutes of relaxing are up.

0755 to 0945 Classes

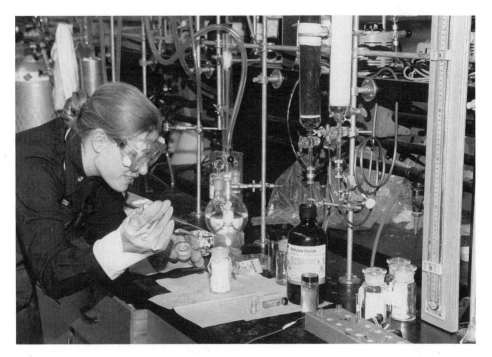

Science plays a big part in every mid's studies at the academy.
U.S. NAVAL ACADEMY

All at once, the academy is filled with midshipmen heading to class. Each class is fifty minutes long, with ten minutes between classes to get to your next one.

Lots of us take courses that offer real hands-on experience. That's because we have top technical equipment here like subsonic and supersonic wind tunnels, a subcritical nuclear reactor, and a twelve-meter satellite earth station that receives transmissions from all over the world. We even have big towing tanks, which is great news if you're interested in things like naval architecture. You can design a boat, build it, and test it. You get on a carriage that travels down the 380-foot tank, watch your boat ride waves as big as three feet, and record how well it does in different conditions.

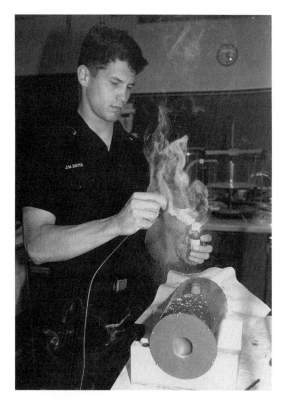

A successful science experiment.

*Midshipmen use towing
tanks to test the boats
they design.*

Computers are everywhere and used by every midshipman.
U.S. NAVAL ACADEMY

We also have fantastic computers. One way I like to use computers is with our war-gaming trainer. It works like this. Twenty people are placed at different computer stations. One person handles missile control, another radar, and so on. The teacher describes a situation. You might be out at sea and a bunch of submarines or aircraft are coming at you. After a while, everyone's yelling at everyone else. It gets very hectic.

It sure is a challenge to work together.

Since this is the Naval Academy, many of us spend a lot of time learning about water. One way we do this is on our large fleet of boats. We have twenty 108-foot yard patrol craft, ninety sailboards, one hundred lasers, twenty-four dinghies, thirty 24-foot Rainbow-class knockabouts, twelve J-24s, twenty 44-foot sloops, and twelve 40- to 60-foot offshore sail training craft.

Everyone learns to sail during plebe summer. You have to be good enough to get a B-level qualification card, which means you can sail boats like lasers or knockabouts by yourself. If you really like to sail, you can compete here on many levels—locally, nationally, even internationally. Of course, some midshipmen sail just for fun, and that's okay too.

Sometimes when I'm sailing I remember when nine of us took a boat down the Chesapeake Bay to the Atlantic Ocean for a five-day sail. I can still feel the salt on my face as I think back . . .

A yard patrol craft. U.S. NAVAL ACADEMY

We're headed toward Bermuda. It's the dead of night. I can feel the weather change. It turns rough. Fourteen-foot seas break against the mast as we surf up and down each wave. One wrong move and we'll be drenched. I'm wet. I'm tired.

It's my turn to change sails as the storm front strengthens. I have to do it. I don't want to, but I don't have a choice. The boat will be destroyed if I don't act fast.

Finally, the wind calms.

As we sail along, surrounded by darkness, I know I'll remember this trip for the rest of my life.

Academy sailboats compete in the popular races in Annapolis.
U.S. NAVAL ACADEMY

Setting sail. U.S. NAVAL ACADEMY

Tripping over a rock brings me back to today. I pick up my step. I don't want to be late for class. You guessed it—that's against the rules.

0955 to 1145 More Classes

Walking to class. U.S. NAVAL ACADEMY

As I walk across the yard to my next class, I worry about how much homework I have to do. Compared to other colleges, our course load is extra big. In addition to regular subjects like history, engineering, science, and math, we also have professional training. We learn about weapons, naval science, electrical engineering, and leadership.

Sometimes professional courses are a pain. You'd rather work hard on courses for your major. But that's not such a good idea. All your grades influence your service assignment—your future. Once again, the pressure's on.

We do get used to working hard. We even work in the summer. This kind of training has been going on since 1845. It's usually a great adventure. Our first summer we go on a sailing cruise, and then we train at Quantico, a Marine base. We train at naval bases and on ships for the next two summers too. Whatever we do, it's always a learning experience, and often exciting. For instance, it's hard to top the thrill of jumping out of a plane for the first time. Thinking back, it was just like this . . .

> *My heart is pumping. I check my equipment again and again. One mistake could mean death for me or for someone else. They've just opened the back doors of the plane. I see the ground speeding by; the wind beats against my legs. I hear the "Stand in the door" command and then, "Go, go, go" in the distance. I'm getting more and more nervous. Finally, it's my turn. I stand in the door and put my hands on the skin of the plane. I look the jump master dead in the eye; he taps me on the shoulder. I jump.*
>
> *I see ground, sky, plane, ground, sky, plane. I'm tossed around like a rag doll. The engine roars in my ears. And then, suddenly, everything is still as my parachute opens and I drop in silence. I close my eyes for a second and then they pop open wide. "I've got to land!"*

Parachute jump training at Norfolk, Virginia. U.S. NAVAL ACADEMY

Parachute jump—the real thing. A U.S. Navy SEAL jumps from a C-130 aircraft. U.S. NAVY

My brain kicks into gear. First, I make sure I don't look down. Then I check the wind and count on my past training to click in. It works. I land, roll, unhook my parachute, pack it all up, and head back.

That was a day I'll never forget. What I can't forget now is formation. That's next. Here I go.

1210 Formation

When the weather isn't good, formation takes place indoors.

Once again, all midshipmen line up in formation by company. This is a formation many tourists come to see. We all look the same to them, but each company is very different. Each has its own personality and carries on traditions that have gone on for years. For instance, Thirteenth Company always relays (by running) the game ball to the Army-Navy football game, often held as far away as Philadelphia or New Jersey. Thirty-fourth Company plays our well-known croquet matches against St. John's College, and Ninth Company paints the Indian figurehead Tecumseh (named for a war-loving Shawnee chief) for special occasions.

Thirteenth Company delivers the game ball after running in a relay all the way from Annapolis! THE LUCKY BAG

Companies also compete all year long to become the Color Company. Everything from good grades and winning at sports to clean rooms and creative decorations on company hallways counts toward who gets to carry the colors. This company represents the academy at important events, carries the American flag, and gets special benefits, like going to an away football game of choice (all expenses paid) or getting some of the best parking spaces at the academy. For some of us, working to be the Color Company really builds company spirit. For others, it's not a big deal.

Always be ready for a personal inspection. U.S. NAVAL ACADEMY

Today, all thirty-six companies look their best. It's time for personal inspection. Everything has to be perfect. Your uniform has to be clean. Anything shiny, like belt buckles and shoes, has to gleam. Your hair has to look just right. The gig line (where the button on your shirt meets your fly) must be straight, and so should the band on your hat. It's called a smile if it's crooked. The crows on your hat buttons have to stand up.

The top of your hat can't be dusty, and neither can your shoes. You probably think you know the right way to polish shoes. That's what I thought too when I first got here. Then I checked out the shoes worn by the upperclass mids. They look like mirrors.

The brim of your hat must be clean—all the time. U.S. NAVAL ACADEMY

Checking for the perfect shoe shine. U.S. NAVAL ACADEMY

*A quick way to measure where the anchor pin goes
is to use a quarter.*

The anchors on your shirt collar have to be placed exactly. To do that you measure with a ruler one inch from the front of the collar and one inch from the bottom of the collar. Women follow the same dress code for neatness. They can also wear one ring on each hand and brushed-gold ball earrings. Female midshipmen can wear only two braids and two barrettes to keep their hair above their collar.

So how do we handle all of these details, the hard times, the pressure? The answer is easy. Friendship. Everyone always says you make your friends for life at the academy. It's true. I know now and in the future, when we're scattered all over the world, I'll be able to call on my friends and they'll be there for me.

Even if we're not good friends, midshipmen help each other out. We all learn during plebe year that you can't make it through this school alone. We need each other whether we like it or not. It's also important to learn to work as a team because that's what we'll have to do in the military some day.

What I need now is lunch. And luckily, it's time to eat.

1220 to 1300 Lunch

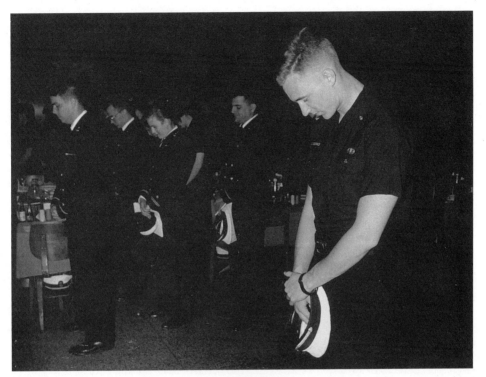

We stand and pray before we eat.

I'm starved. I watch as the plebes rig our table by opening cartons, taking covers off the butter, and making sure everything is set up just right.

When we hear the command "Brigade seats," we sit down in order of our class. Plebes sit last. We eat with our company, but we sit in groups of twelve, called squads. Each squad is supposed to have three people from each class year, but it's not always exact.

Today we're having the most popular lunch here—chicken tenders. The menu also features mashed potatoes, salad, and cannonballs. These are big apple dumplings served with a very sweet sauce. There is a tradition here called The Cannonball Run. A plebe makes a bargain with an upperclass mid that he can eat twelve cannonballs after eating a complete meal. If the plebe wins, he might not have to do daily rates for a week. At every table we also always have peanut butter and jelly, in case you don't like the meal.

The way we eat keeps us in good shape. We're very concerned about calories, fat, and cholesterol. You're not allowed to be overweight at the academy, which is why we get weighed every six months.

In King Hall the mood is relaxed, but some rules still apply. For instance, plebes can only walk down the wide center aisle. Second class has the added privilege of walking in the aisles between tables. First class can walk anywhere, including the outside edge (called First-Class Alley). Actually, these rules make it easy for everyone to move around. We also have to stay at meals for at least ten minutes.

Time for chow.

As we eat, I think about all the people who have sat at these tables before us. President Jimmy Carter, Alan Shepard (the first American astronaut in space), Rear Adm. Richard E. Byrd (a famous North and South Pole explorer), Fleet Adm. Chester W. Nimitz of World War II fame, football players Napoleon McCallum and Roger Staubach, the basketball star David Robinson, celebrity Montel Williams, and many others.

Many boys, like this one, were awed in the early 1960s when Fleet Admiral Nimitz visited their towns. U.S. NAVAL INSTITUTE COLLECTION

Talk show host Montel Williams during a return visit to the academy.
U.S. NAVAL ACADEMY

*Comdr. Alan B.
Shepard, Jr., in 1961.*
U.S. NAVY

*Adm. Richard E. Byrd
smokes his corncob
pipe at his old stove.*
U.S. NAVY

David Robinson scores. DOD/U.S. AIR FORCE

Sitting here in the comfort of King Hall, just like those famous men once did, I know something they knew too. If the time ever comes when I have to make any sacrifice for my country, even my life, I'm ready. It's my job. I think about the guts it takes to be a real leader. I imagine that some day it may be my turn to fight for my country. My dessert rests on my fork as I picture myself in the heat of battle . . .

We're behind enemy lines, ready to meet the enemy eye to eye. I look around at my troops. I know we're all trained to be the best, but if anyone messes up, it's my fault. I may have to tell them to

*Death is a part of military reality. Midshipmen are ready to serve—
and even die for—their country.* U.S. COAST GUARD

*do something that might get them killed. We're ready for any-
thing, even the fear that we feel right now.*
   I hear gunfire in the distance, getting closer and closer.

Speaking of getting closer, it's time for training, which follows
lunchtime. On the schedule for this afternoon is financial plan-
ning. Often we use this time to learn about subjects like computers,
or to discuss important issues. Some days we have no training at
all. Then we get to do something great—whatever we want!

1330 to 1525 Still More Classes

I walk across the yard to my afternoon classes with my friend Katy. She laughs as she tells me about a comment she overheard recently. A tourist in Annapolis saw her and said, "There goes a girl one."

"I guess no matter how long we've been here, we still stand out," sighs Katy.

"I think it would be hard to be a woman here," I add.

"Sometimes it is," Katy replies, turning serious. "The truth is, everything you do is magnified. So the good looks great and the bad looks pretty bad."

"Does it feel weird to be the only woman in a classroom?" I ask.

Juliane Gallina was the first female to become the Naval Academy's highest ranking midshipman—brigade commander—in the fall of 1992.

U.S. NAVAL ACADEMY

Margaret Morrison was brigade commander in the fall of 1995.
U.S. NAVAL ACADEMY

"You get used to it. In some ways it's great. You feel like you have lots of friendly, protective brothers," Katy adds, giving me a shove.

"Isn't there anything you don't like?" I ask, pushing back.

"Uniforms! What we get to wear isn't that flattering."

"You know, a lot of midshipmen didn't like the idea of women coming here when they were first admitted in 1976," I say.

"Some still don't," moans Katy, rolling her eyes. "But I think most of us are accepted for who we are. Let's face it. We've held the top midshipman position of brigade commander. We've proven we can succeed, right?"

"Right. Actually, doing well here is hard for just about everybody. Sometimes it really gets to me."

"I know what you mean," Katy nods. "The pressure of sports, classes, training, and . . ."

I interrupt, laughing. "Cleaning our rooms!"

About four times a semester we clean our rooms and wax the decks. Our efforts get a grade. Tomorrow's a big test.

I probably don't have to tell you this is no ordinary room cleaning. First, remember the words "dust free." There can't be any anywhere, not even on your shoes. And let me tell you, those doing the inspecting do their best to find it. They turn over desks, check the top of the doors, and take off radiator covers. They check the coffin (an open space under the mattress where you can store things). They even check the door bolt to see if there's dust inside that.

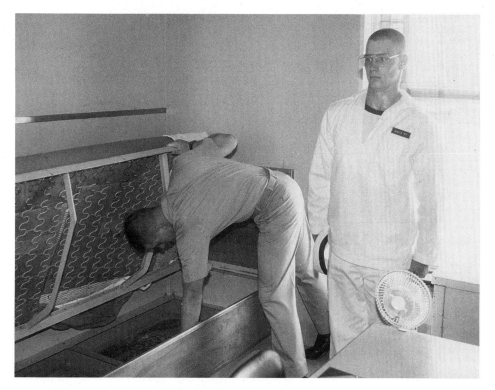

Checking in the coffin (under the bed) for dust. U.S. NAVAL ACADEMY

Something isn't quite right. U.S. NAVAL ACADEMY

Wastebaskets must be empty and linens clean. Pillows have to be folded just the right way. Beds can't be wrinkled and must have a six-inch collar (that's the place where you fold your sheet over at the head of the bed). They have to be made with perfect forty-five-degree hospital corners.

Just to show you how picky the midshipmen doing the inspections get, they take a black sock and wipe it across the shower. If it picks up any soap scum, that's a "hit," the word for a demerit that lowers your grade from a perfect 4.0.

Of course, our rooms are always supposed to be neat, clean, and ready for inspections. Attention to detail prepares us for peak readiness in times of war. It instills in us a good "fighting edge." And then there's the practical side. Living together in a big group

Passing the white-glove test. U.S. NAVAL ACADEMY

at the academy means we've got to clean to keep away illness, mice, snakes, and bugs!

Room cleaning isn't fun, but like all things here, you do what you have to do to get the job done. It was like that during summer Marine Corps training, which we all do after our second year here. We had to go through tough obstacle courses. Crawling through the mud wasn't my idea of fun, but I had no choice. I can still feel that mud, and smell it . . .

I pull myself through the blackest, dirtiest water I've ever seen. The smell is awful; I can hardly breathe. I can't believe all four of us have to make it over a seventy-foot-high cliff that goes up at a ninety-degree angle. It takes incredible strength, but we do it. Then I see the lake ahead. I know there are snakes under its muddy surface. As we make our way across the lake, the water comes up to eye level. We're holding our rifles above our heads.

It's not easy for anyone, but we help each other out. "You can do it. You've got what it takes," we tell each other. And it works. We find the strength to keep going.

Katy gives me a nudge. "You still here?"

"Sorry. I was just thinking about last summer."

"Don't torture yourself," she teases. "See you later."

I wave goodbye and pick up my step. If I don't get to class I may not pass my course in navigation. That's one obstacle I don't want to encounter.

Training puts midshipmen to the test.

Midshipmen go through summer training at Quantico Marine Base.

Midshipmen like the words "Pass in review" because that means the drill practice is almost over.

1530 to 1800 Sports and Drills

It's time to either drill or practice sports. When we drill (during spring and fall), we spend hours learning to march with rifles and bayonets. We follow the orders "Right shoulder arms. Left shoulder arms. Present arms. Parade rest." We feel proud; we look good. A few of us also feel something else—BORED. It can be very uncomfortable standing in the sweltering hot sun, feeling sticky. At formal parades they actually have a medical team on hand in case anyone faints.

Drilling isn't popular. We do it because we have to. Three of our favorite words are "Pass in review." That command means that after standing for hours, we get to march and be done.

The mids are finally ready for a formal parade. U.S. NAVAL ACADEMY

When we're not drilling, we're playing sports. Physical fitness is almost as important as good grades. Playing a sport is required. Of course, it's pretty easy to find something you like. We've got everything here. If you don't play a varsity sport, you can play intramurals, like volleyball or racquetball. Every season there are three or four intramurals you can choose from. This place is an athlete's dream. We even have a golf course and an indoor ice-skating rink.

The sport that gets the most attention is football. Army-Navy games are big events. The two schools have been big rivals since they first played together in 1890. Navy won that day, 24 to 0.

The last academic week of the fall leads up to the big Army-Navy game. We call this Army Week, and it's a time when most midshipmen don't sleep. They're having too much fun. Plebes are

Football is very important at the academy. U.S. NAVAL ACADEMY

Bill the Goat was kidnapped by West Point cadets one year, and the midshipmen got even in 1991 by "borrowing" Army's mules for a couple of days. U.S. NAVAL ACADEMY

often found under the tables at King Hall leaving a blob of peanut butter or honey on someone's perfectly shined shoe. And whoops! Who squeezed that bottle of baby powder all over what *was* a clean dark uniform?

By the way, have you met Bill the Goat? He's been the team mascot since the fourth Army-Navy game, which was played in 1893. Naturally, we won, and Bill has been our lucky hero ever since.

Attendance at all home games is required. To get to the stadium where the game is played, we line up and march in a parade through the streets of Annapolis. Once we get there, we sit together

It's fun to shout and get into the spirit at football games. U.S. NAVAL ACADEMY

and cheer our team on. When we score, plebes go down on the field and do push-ups to match the total number of points. Lots of parties and events go along with the games.

What also goes along with games is plebes against the upper classes in guessing the scores of upcoming games. If the plebe guesses right, he or she might get to listen to the radio in an upperclass mid's room for a few hours. If the plebe is wrong? Shining shoes, folding laundry, or reading poetry to a tree might be the penalty.

I learned an interesting football fact the other day. In 1891, midshipman Joseph Reeves wore the first protective headgear seen on an American football field. He had an Annapolis merchant make one for him out of leather. I guess you could say he's the inventor of the first football helmet.

One more sports tradition here is bell ringing. At the end of each athletic season, the brigade gathers in Tecumseh Court. Team members and coaches ring the Enterprise Bell. For victory over Army, the bell is rung from the time the results of the game are known in Bancroft Hall until the team returns home.

In addition to playing organized sports, we have to pass personal physical-readiness tests every semester. We are timed doing push-ups and curl-ups (two minutes for each). Men have to do a minimum of forty push-ups; women have to do a minimum of eighteen. Men and women both have to do a minimum of sixty-five curl-ups. We are also timed on a 1.5-mile run. Maximum time for men is ten minutes, thirty seconds; for women, twelve minutes, forty seconds. If there's some reason you can't run, you can substitute a swim test. The scores from all of these tests are combined for a total grade.

A few of our sports, like boxing, wrestling, and judo, are new to some midshipmen. A lot of people have never been aggressive before, but they quickly learn how to take a punch. You find out you're tougher than you think. Our physical requirements are hard, but so are many of our future jobs, where long hours in tough situations demand strength.

There's one requirement that's extra hard here for many of us. It's called the Tower Jump. We do it off the pool diving platform

Plebes do push-ups to match the score. U.S. NAVAL ACADEMY

*Every mid works hard—sometimes gritting your teeth helps—
to stay in good shape.* U.S. NAVAL ACADEMY/P. SALESI

that is ten-meters high. The pool looks awfully far down when you stand up there. To some people, this is like jumping off the end of the world.

Naturally, the jump is supposed to prepare you for the future. I asked my friend Sarah, sarcastically, what this jump could do for me.

"Just think about being a SEAL," she replied. "Think about practicing a waterborne insertion."

That's exactly what I did when it was my turn to take the plunge. I closed my eyes and pictured this . . .

It's time to drop. Six of us are dangling below a Marine Corps helicopter on a rope ladder. The helicopter can't land; we have to jump to the river below. It looks so far down. And it is. Somewhere around sixty feet. My knees shake as I anticipate the fall. And then I remember. Hey, I've done the Tower Jump. Of course, that was only half as high, but it helps me get a grip on myself now. Well, here goes.

At times, jumping into the pool is fun. After their last parade ever as midshipmen, firsties celebrate by taking the plunge from the tower.
BOB GILBERT

I'm not sure thinking about the future helped, but I didn't have much choice about making the jump. (Actually, I did. Last year, the jump was required. This year, I could choose between three platforms—10 meters, 7.5 meters, or 5 meters—but the height of the platform affects your grade, and I needed help. So, it was the ten-meter jump for me.)

1700 to 1900 Dinner

Dinner is a casual buffet. There's always a salad bar, and tonight there's a potato bar too. Pasta is popular around here. On the menu is lasagna, along with green beans, French bread, and lemon cheesecake.

This is definitely the calmest meal of the day. We talk about almost everything. One minute we're laughing about a scene in a funny movie, and the next minute we're debating about nuclear war. As always, plebes can't jump into the conversation. They can speak to upperclass mids only when spoken to.

Tonight the subject of breaking rules comes up. There are millions of things you can get in trouble for. You can't "mouth off" (talk back) or say "I'm not going to do that." You can't be late for anything. You can't miss an event or a class.

Punishments can be light or heavy. You might have to undergo extra uniform inspections, for example, or you could lose your liberty (freedom to leave the academy). You could lose privileges like driving a car on the yard (you can keep a car here your last year) or wearing civilian clothes. Of course, if you've done something really bad, you could even get thrown out of school.

But we're not perfect. A lot of us have done something that's against the rules (of course, some never do).

One of the biggest no-no's is going over the wall. This is a tradition that's gone on *forever*. It means leaving the academy when you're not supposed to. I guess it's a way of saying, "I've gotta break out of this place." Not many try this because if you get caught, you pay the consequences. Many who go over the wall just do it to put up a poster that might say "Beat Army." That probably won't get you in too much trouble. If you get caught hanging out in Annapolis, you're in BIG TROUBLE.

Inside the academy, many places are off-limits. One is called the Crystal Palace. It's on the roof of Bancroft Hall. I've heard that when the famous Admiral Nimitz was here, he and his friends also found a way to go up to the roof and have fun—just like we do.

On Hundred's Night—100 days before commissioning—upperclass mids switch places with plebes, who might order them to do silly stunts just for fun.
U.S. NAVAL ACADEMY

The Ho Chi Minh Trail is also forbidden. It's a network of underground steam pipes and tunnels where midshipmen sometimes play after lights out. Midshipmen have been doing this for a hundred years. When you go down into these catacombs, you see graffiti like "Joe was here April 2, 1942." It's cool.

Something that's not supposed to happen—but does anyway, during Army Week—is called the "Wild Man." A plebe pours a pitcher of water on an upperclassman, and if that plebe can make it back to his or her room, the plebe is safe. If caught? The upperclassman decides the consequences.

There is one tradition that's not really against the rules, even though it takes place late at night. It happens during football season, like this . . .

Pep rallies get everyone in the mood for the big football games.
U.S. NAVAL ACADEMY

Staying up late, relaxing, and letting off some steam.
U.S. NAVAL ACADEMY

*I open one eye. I'm half asleep, but I hear footsteps in the hall.
Then I know it's the plebes. They're waking us up for a pep rally.*

*I hit the decks with everyone else and head for Tecumseh Court.
When we get there, plebes are dressed in whatever they could get
their hands on. They wear bathrobes, bandanas on their heads,
and camouflage paint on their faces. Some have shaving cream
in hand. The drum and bugle corps joins in. Music fills the air,
and so do our shouts and laughing. It feels good to let loose.*

By the next morning everything is cleaned up. We're not in
trouble. These pep rallies are preplanned. There's even a speaker
system set up outside for music. It's against the rules to be out after
lights out, but in this case that rule is ignored. What's important is
that everyone had a great time. We're all pumped up and ready for
the game.

Halloween is a great time for pranks and fun.
THE *LUCKY BAG*

Of course, other fun things are allowed too. We have dances, we hang out in Annapolis a lot, and many of us have families we're close to in this city. Plebe year, every midshipman is assigned a sponsor. For many midshipmen, the sponsoring family provides a home away from home, a place to relax, for all four years.

The ring dance is a special event for members of the second class. They finally get to wear their class rings, which they dip into a bowl that contains water from all the seven seas. U.S. NAVAL ACADEMY

We also have concerts. Bands like the Beach Boys, the Temptations, Chicago, the Moody Blues, INXS, and Mary Chapin Carpenter have performed here for us.

I'd much rather think about having fun than all the work I have to do tonight. But wait! It's time for ECA (extracurricular activity time), and I've got a club meeting to go to. After dinner, clubs—more than seventy of them—meet. Many clubs are related to sports, our majors, or fun hobbies such as singing, scuba diving, and photography. I'm sure glad I have something to do before hitting the books tonight.

1915 Study Time

Mids spend a lot of time studying.

It's time to study, study, study. Plebes have about twenty hours of homework a week; upperclass midshipmen have about thirty. By now you know, making it academically is tough. That's one reason we have Tecumseh. Since 1917, he's been considered the god of the 2.0 (passing grade). Before exams, midshipmen throw pennies at him, hoping to land one in his quiver (where his arrows are kept). If we do, we're supposed to pass the test.

Tecumseh is for luck; the library is for studying. It's quiet there, and *big*. There are more than 600,000 books on the shelves!

Many evenings, when I've walked back to my room from the library, I've worried about whether or not I could make it here. Most of us feel this way at some time or another. When the pressure gets bad, I've seen people get pretty depressed. I've found that a quick cure for feeling down is to go for a walk. I try to notice

Tecumseh is the god of good grades and good luck in sporting events. He also gets painted on many occasions. He's been everything from a skeleton and the grim reaper to a Teenage Mutant Ninja Turtle and Spiderman.

U.S. NAVAL ACADEMY

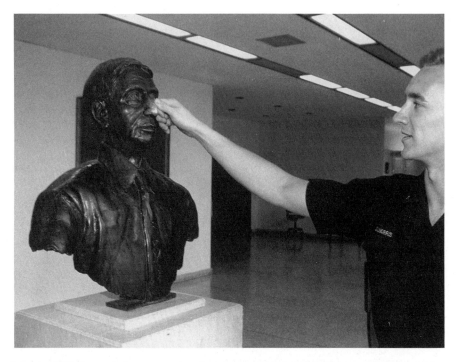

Admiral Rickover's bronze nose is always kept shiny from all the rubbing it gets for good luck before exams.

every detail of the academy. So many buildings are old. (This place is actually a historic landmark.) Statues dot the yard, gifts from recent classes and classes that graduated long ago. I read the street signs and cross over playing fields. They're all named after someone important.

Then, all of a sudden, I feel a connection with thousands of midshipmen who have walked where I'm walking right now. It helps to know they made it through this place. If they could do it, so can I.

That's one way to reduce stress. I smile when I think about another way we let off some steam. Often, during exam week, it goes something like this . . .

I glance at the clock. It's 0200 (two o'clock in the morning!). I've been stuck on an impossible math problem for hours. I can't fig-ure it out. I'm ready to scream. I walk to the window, throw it

Playing football in the halls is one way mids relax at night.

*open, stick my head out, and yell as loud as I can. Within minutes,
there's a chain reaction. Everyone is hanging out the windows of
Bancroft Hall, yelling. I can see more than two thousand windows,
and only four or five are dark, with the lights off. I feel better now
and ready to get back to the books.*

*Every company has its own wardroom where mids hang out.
Plebes are not allowed.*

Tonight, as I go back to my room after a long evening at the
library, I'm beat. But as I walk into my company, I find myself in
the middle of a "splashdown." That's when plebes let loose and
dance in the halls for about an hour. These events are arranged by
the upperclasses to give the plebes a break. I think I'll hang out in
our company's wardroom (a place where we can relax, snack, and
watch TV), which is off-limits to plebes.

2400 Taps

It's midnight, and time for taps, which means we've all got to be back in Mother B with our companies. Plebe taps was at 2300. After their required nightly singing of the "Navy Blue and Gold," it's lights out for them. Upperclass midshipmen can stay up as late as they want. Tonight I'm tired and ready for bed. I close my eyes. Looking back over my time here, I remember how homesick I was as a plebe. I often felt sad and lonely, cut off from the outside world, so far away from friends and family. I think about how far I've come. It feels good to push myself hard. Yet sometimes it seems like too much. And then there's service assignment still ahead of me. What if I don't get what I want?

My worries float away as I remember why I chose to come to the academy: I'm here to become an officer. And no matter what I end up doing, whether it's on shore, doing all the paperwork, or being on the front lines, trading bullets with the enemy, it will be my job and a dream come true.

As I drift off toward sleep, an old memory awakens. I can see myself clearly. I was just ten years old . . .

My shoes click against the pavement. I stand tall, march straight, and pretend this is my school. As we tour the Naval Academy, my parents walk at my side, but I ignore them. Turning a corner, I see hundreds of midshipmen going to class. I notice every detail of their uniforms. They look like they're all going somewhere important. I can't take my eyes off them.

For the rest of the day, I have butterflies in my stomach. And then I know why. I realize that some day, some way, I want to be a midshipman too. I hope I have what it takes. I hope, I hope . . .

As I slip into my dreams, it feels good to know that some wishes do come true.

Dreams can come true for all boys and girls who hope to come to the Naval Academy some day.

ABOUT THE AUTHOR

Sandra Travis-Bildahl has been a magazine, television, radio, and advertising writer for more than fifteen years. Formerly a producer for the radio program "The Subject Is Young People" hosted by Bob Keeshan (better known as Captain Kangaroo), this award-winning writer is currently working on several projects for children.

Ms. Travis-Bildahl lives in Annapolis, Maryland, with her husband and two children.

The **Naval Institute Press** is the book-publishing arm of the U.S. Naval Institute, a private, nonprofit society for sea service professionals and others who share an interest in naval and maritime affairs. Established in 1873 at the U.S. Naval Academy in Annapolis, Maryland, where its offices remain today, the Naval Institute has more than 85,000 members worldwide.

Members of the Naval Institute receive the influential monthly magazine *Proceedings* and discounts on fine nautical prints and on ship and aircraft photos. They also have access to the transcripts of the Institute's Oral History Program and get discounted admission to any of the Institute-sponsored seminars offered around the country. Discounts are also available to the colorful bimonthly magazine *Naval History*.

The Naval Institute's book-publishing program, begun in 1898 with basic guides to naval practices, has broadened its scope in recent years to include books of more general interest. Now the Naval Institute Press publishes about 100 titles each year, ranging from how-to books on boating and navigation to battle histories, biographies, ship and aircraft guides, and novels. Institute members receive discounts of 20 to 50 percent on the Press's nearly 600 books in print.

Full-time students are eligible for special half-price membership rates. Life memberships are also available.

For a free catalog describing Naval Institute Press books currently available, and for further information about joining the U.S. Naval Institute, please write to:

Membership Department
U.S. Naval Institute
118 Maryland Avenue
Annapolis, Maryland 21402-5035

Telephone: (800) 233-8764
Fax: (410) 269-7940